STRANGE
and
CURIOUS
CREATURES

RUPERT OLIVER

Illustrated by BERNARD LONG

HODDER AND STOUGHTON
LONDON SYDNEY AUCKLAND TORONTO

King of
Saxony

Red plumed

Wilson's

Magnificent

British Library Cataloguing in Publication Data
Oliver, Rupert
    Strange and curious creatures.
    1. Animals—Juvenile literature
    I. Title   II. Long, Bernard
    591   QL49

ISBN 0–340–34718–X

First published 1984
Published by Hodder and Stoughton Children's Books,
a division of Hodder and Stoughton Ltd, Mill Road,
Dunton Green, Sevenoaks, Kent TN13 2YJ.

Printed in Belgium

Contents

Some of the most beautiful birds in the world belong to the family Birds of Paradise. See page 48.

Superb

Strange and Curious Creatures

Australia has some of the world's strangest mammals. Above is the Kangaroo and Duck-billed platypus.

Outback Oddities

The great island continent of Australia has been isolated from the rest of the world for many millions of years. This has allowed it to evolve its own peculiar wildlife, two of the strangest examples of which are shown above.

The Red Kangaroo is one of the largest of the kangaroos, standing about one and a half metres tall and weighing almost thirty kilogrammes.

Some other kangaroos are as small as mice and are known as rat kangaroos.

The most striking thing about the kangaroos is the way that they move about. They hop. Living out in the open spaces of the Australian Outback, the Red Kangaroo has managed to bring this method of travel to a peak of perfection. The powerful hind legs of this creature can drive it along at speeds approaching fifty kilometres an hour, covering ten metres with each bound.

While the kangaroo is hopping, the heavy tail acts as a counterweight, balancing the body and head. But when the creature is at rest, the tail is just as useful, acting as a third leg on which the kangaroo can put its weight.

The other most noticeable thing about the kangaroo is that it keeps its young in a pouch. This odd behaviour is shared by all marsupials, a group of mammals which lives mainly in Australia. When the young is born it is blind, hairless and quite helpless. The tiny creature, which only weighs one gram, crawls up its mother's fur and into the pouch, where it finds warmth, milk and safety. After several months, the young kangaroo starts to venture out and fend for itself, but it will still return to its mother's pouch at the first sign of trouble.

When early explorers first brought back skins of the small creature in our illustration, scientists thought that they were hoaxes. But they were not fakes. They belonged to a Duckbilled Platypus. This small creature is one of the enigmas of the animal world. It has fur like a mammal, a bill like a bird and yet lays eggs like a reptile. After many years scientists decided that it was a mammal, but that it belonged to a very primitive group known as the monotremes.

This fifty-centimetre-long creature spends much of its time in the water searching for the larvae and small fish on which it feeds. When it dives under the water, the platypus is able to seal off its eyes and ears with flaps of skin so that no water can get into them.

The eggs, of which there are usually two, are laid in a cosy nest at the far end of the burrow which the platypus digs out of the river banks. After ten days the young platypuses hatch out into a nest lined with leaves in which they stay for the first four months of their lives. It is very unusual for a mammal to lay eggs. In fact only one other mammal has been known to do so.

Another unusual feature among mammals that is found in the platypus is venom. The hind legs of the males carry sharp spikes which are connected to a venom gland and can cause an ugly wound.

These two unique creatures make up only a tiny fraction of the highly unusual and diverse fauna found in Australia.

9

The Slow One

A creature whose name has become synonymous with laziness is the sloth from South America.

This slow moving mammal spends all its life hanging in the trees, using its strong clawed feet to hold on to the branches. If, for any reason, it should fall to the ground, the sloth would be almost helpless. But up in the branches, it is an expert, if rather sluggish climber, able to move with ease through the tangle of vegetation.

The large claws of the sloth are a feature of the edentates, the group of mammals to which the sloth and several other creatures in this book belong. Another feature of the edentates is the presence of degenerate, that is, small and weak, teeth. This is particularly evident in the three-toed sloth, while the two-toed species has two pairs of large, sharp premolars.

The fur of this docile beast is also an interesting feature. Because the sloth spends most of its time upside down, the long fur grows from the belly to the back, whereas most animals have fur growing the other way. Each strand of hair has minute grooves running along its entire length. Into these grooves settle microscopic plants, called algae. This gives a green sheen to the animal, a peculiar trait which helps the sloth to evade its enemies. By staying absolutely still, the greenish animal will blend into the vegetation and become almost invisible.

Though this creature may be difficult to find in the dense undergrowth, its incredible life-style is well worthy of close study.

Slow but very sure is the Sloth as it moves through the dense vegetation of the South American trees.

10

The African Sprinter

The sloth may be the slowest of the mammals, but quite the opposite is true of the cheetah. This remarkable member of the cat family can reach the staggering speed of approximately 100 kilometres an hour.

The need for this quite extraordinary turn of speed is not difficult to understand. On the vast, open grassy plains there is little or no cover for the cheetah when it hunts its prey. For this reason, the cheetah cannot hunt in the same way as do other large cats, that is by creeping up on its prey and making a surprise attack. Any gazelle out on the plains would be able to see a cheetah approaching long before the cat was able to catch it. The only hope for the cheetah is that it can run faster than its prey and overtake it.

In the course of thousands of generations, the cheetah has evolved into a creature built almost exclusively for speed. Its lightness of build and small head reduce the weight which the muscles of the cheetah has to drive across the plains. The long legs obviously help to lengthen the stride, and therefore increase the speed, but a less obvious aid to the stride is the backbone. The spinal column of the cheetah is remarkably flexible. By arching its back at the right moment, the cheetah can draw its legs right up underneath the body or spread them far out in front.

The end result of all these special adaptations is a cat capable of running down virtually any prey it chooses from those creatures roaming the plains.

In Africa lives one of the fastest moving members of the cat family. The Cheetah is also known as the "hunting leopard."

11

The Hunter and the Hunted

In the world of the insect a momentary lack of vigilance can prove fatal. Almost any insect is a potential meal for another creature.

Some insects protect themselves by having a sting and others by ejecting a foul-tasting substance to put off attackers. But perhaps the most effective means of survival, certainly the most used, is simply to avoid being seen by a predator in the first place.

To this end many insects have evolved so as to be the same colour as their surroundings, be they green, brown or black. The best concealed of all must surely be the leaf insect. There are, in fact, many dozens of types of leaf insect, only one of which is illustrated here but they all have several features in common.

Most striking of all is that they are not only coloured green to blend in with the leaves but they are also shaped like leaves. Some leaf insects even have markings similar to the veins on a leaf, enabling them to merge into their surroundings more effectively.

It is this remarkable similarity to a leaf which earned these strange creatures their common name, and which has ensured their survival in a harsh world.

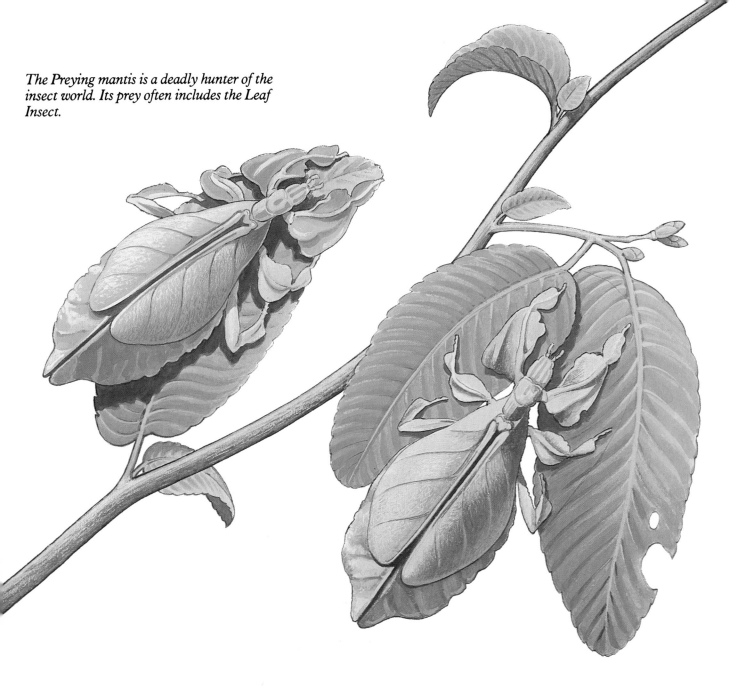

The Preying mantis is a deadly hunter of the insect world. Its prey often includes the Leaf Insect.

Camouflage is also used by another creature, the preying mantis, not to escape predators but to catch prey. This creature uses its camouflage in a cunning way. It remains absolutely motionless, hidden against the leaves by its green colour, until its sharp eyes catch sight of another insect. Then, in a lightning movement, it will strike.

The preying mantis is a specialised creature, dedicated to eating other insects. Its eyes are very large and efficient. They are able to train on to a hunted insect by using a highly manoeuvrable neck, which is a rare feature amongst insects.

The curious stance of the mantis is not only essential to its hunting activities, it is also responsible for its name. It struck entomologists that it looked like a priest at prayer. So, punning the words praying and preying, the creature was named the preying mantis. Mantis means priest.

The forelegs, which are drawn up under the insect's head, are deadly weapons. When the mantis has spotted an insect within range, it will shoot out its forelegs until they reach the hapless victim and then snap them shut. This has the effect of trapping the prey in a vice-like grip from which there is no escape.

Though this deadly hunter is no friend to the insects on which it feeds, it is of enormous help to man, for it kills many harmful insects which would otherwise destroy crops.

When the preying mantis and the leaf insect meet, the leaf insect would be well advised to keep extra still.

sight of the two eyes looking in opposite directions at the same time. However, once an eye has located an insect the chameleon will slowly but deliberately turn its head and train its other eye on to the target. Once the chameleon has the insect in view with both eyes, it will calculate the distance between it and its prey, ready for the attack.

When this attack comes, it is with lightning speed. In an instant the chameleon shoots out its long sticky tongue to score a direct hit on its prey. Once it has caught the insect, the chameleon will withdraw its tongue, bringing the insect back with it. This extraordinary tongue may measure half the length of the lizard itself.

Incidentally, the well known ability of the chameleons to change colour is now believed to be due to changes in temperature and emotions rather than a conscious attempt at camouflage.

The Jackson's Chameleon, left, uses its long tongue to snatch up its unsuspecting victim.

The Chameleon

The fearsome looking beast above is a member of a group of African lizards which has become very specialised for a life in the trees: the chameleon.

When hunting, the chameleon employs many of the peculiar features for which it is famed. A prowling chameleon will never actually stride forward towards its chosen prey. Instead it uses a peculiar swaying gait, moving half a step forwards, then back again before completing the stride. Though this apparently pointless behaviour may seem to slow the lizard down to half speed, it is of vital importance to its hunting technique. The slow swaying motion is a cunning form of camouflage, for it serves to blend the chameleon into the background of swaying leaves and branches.

The eyes of the chameleon, which it uses to find its food, are perhaps the most disconcerting feature of this lizard. They are located in protruding turrets, one on either side of the head. Instead of working together, the eyes move independently. This produces the odd

14

The Last Dragon

The huge three metre long lizard pictured below is known today as the Komodo dragon, after the island of Komodo in Indonesia, where the dragon lives.

Early travellers to the islands found tales of a huge lizard able to bring down fully grown pigs a little hard to believe, and dismissed them as mere rumours. The natives though, knew what they were talking about. Such a feat is well within the capabilities of this creature.

Set upon its powerful and very well developed legs, this large lizard is surprisingly active and can work up a good speed when in pursuit of a meal. Its alertness, together with a powerful set of jaws, means that the dragon is able to feed on a wide selection of the animals on the island. This lizard is truly a creature to be feared.

Below is shown the largest lizard in the world. It is the three-metre long Komodo dragon.

The Frilled lizard, above and on the cover, erects its frill to scare off attackers.

The Deceitful Lizard

The frightening, almost prehistoric, appearance of the creature to be seen above and on the cover of this book, is really just one enormous bluff.

The frilled lizard normally leads a quiet life, poking around in its Australian habitat looking for food and not appearing much different from any other lizard. If, however, it is threatened it will rear up in the air, open its mouth in a most ferocious manner, and erect its frill.

This sudden and dramatic display – the frill is thirty centimetres across – is usually enough to frighten off any predator which considers this metre long lizard an easy meal. Should the frill and gaping mouth not deter a predator, the frilled lizard will take to its heels and run, thus revealing itself to be the opposite of the fierce creature it has tried to portray.

The Building Insects

The appearance of any one of the 1,700 species of termite is not remarkable at all. In fact they are so similar to ants that termites are often known as white ants. What is peculiar to termites is the degree of sophistication of their social lives.

Every so often a termite nest will produce a swarm of flying termites. In each swarm are to be found both king and queen termites which pair off and fly away from the nest. Some may travel surprising distances in their search for a suitable nest site while others may never find one. When a royal couple have located a suitable site, a log, clump of grass or patch of sand, depending on the species, they will land and instantly shed their wings. They will never fly again.

Now that a nest site has been found, the royal couple begin to build and to lay eggs. Gradually the termite colony starts to take shape. It is one of the most fantastic feats of co-operation in the animal kingdom.

The eggs which the queen first lays do not hatch into more royal termites, but into the other classes of insect: workers and soldiers.

As the name suggests, worker termites are the creatures which do all the work of running the nest and it is these which are most often seen. The workers are small, about one and a half centimetres long, and wingless. They are responsible for finding food and bringing it back to the nest, where it will be fed to the developing larvae. Workers also have the job of building, maintaining and extending the nest.

Soldier termites on the other hand, only have one job, to protect the colony. To make sure that they can do this effectively, the soldiers are armed with strong jaws and large heads. Taken together, these two adaptations mean that soldiers are capable of defending themselves successfully against any other insect of their own size and many which are larger.

The object of the workers' attention and the

Tiny though Termites may be, their nests can be twice the height of man.

soldiers' protection is the nest. In many species this is simply a hollowed out log but in some the nests are impressive structures. In colonies which have been established for some time, the tower type of nest may reach an incredible four or five metres high, as can be seen on the left.

These nests are not only big, they are also very complex. Miles of passages twist about inside them, connecting food storage areas, egg incubating areas and other areas needed for the life of the colony. Many of the larger nests have an ingenious air conditioning system built into them. As most termites live in the tropics, their nests could become very hot and stuffy. To combat this a series of interconnecting tunnels is constructed in the walls of the nest. These tunnels ensure that every part of the nest is reached by a draught of fresh air from outside. As the sun beats

There are two classes of Termites, the soldiers whose task it is to protect the nest, and the workers who build, maintain and extend the huge nest.

down on the nest the passages near the nest walls heat up. As the air in these tunnels gets warmer, it rises and drags fresh air in at the base of the nest. In this way the air is kept circulating.

Some termites even include fungus gardens in their nests where fungus is grown for food.

All in all, the termites must be considered among the most socially complex of all insects.

17

The Jungle Army

Tramping across South America can be found another social insect, but this creature has a far more sinister reputation than the wood-eating termite. It is the army ant.

Like the termite, large numbers of these insects live together – anything up to 150,000 of them in an army. Unlike the termites, they are not tied to one location. In fact it is essential to the ants' lifestyle that they move around.

The hordes of army ants move across the jungle like some great black tide. It is unfortunate for any small animal which gets in their way. The ants are predatory and any insect in their path is set upon and devoured. Even small reptiles and mammals are not safe because the ants can attack in such numbers that they are irresistible.

The army marches across the jungle, bringing death and destruction in its wake for seventeen days. Then it stops. For the next twenty days the army rests under a log or in some other sheltered place. During this time eggs are laid, larvae raised and losses made good.

After this break, the army ants reform their column and set off again on their never-ending quest for food.

The Underground Hunter

Though the most familiar way in which a spider traps its insect food is by spinning a web, it is by no means the only method spiders use.

Perhaps the most spectacular trap is that used by the trapdoor spider, which can be seen on the right. This spider will find a suitable piece of ground and start to dig. Eventually it will have constructed a tube-like tunnel, lined with silk. The top of the tunnel is closed off by a hinged lid, which is almost invisible from above. Around the top of the tunnel the spider will have spun a web of silk which lies upon the ground. Once it is inside the tunnel, with the trapdoor closed, and the threads from the web held under its legs, the spider is ready.

When an insect wanders near to the trapdoor, it will inevitably tread on part of the silken web on the ground. The vibrations this sets up in the tunnel alerts the waiting spider to the presence of a potential meal. When the spider judges that the insect is close enough to the trapdoor, it will strike. With amazing speed, the spider opens the trapdoor and seizes its prey in its strong fangs.

The unfortunate victim is injected with poison and then dragged down into the tunnel, and the trapdoor closed behind it. The spider is now able to take its meal in peace.

Spiders do not actually chew their food. Once an insect is caught, it is injected with digestive juices which soften its insides to mush. This mush is then sucked up by the spider and fully digested.

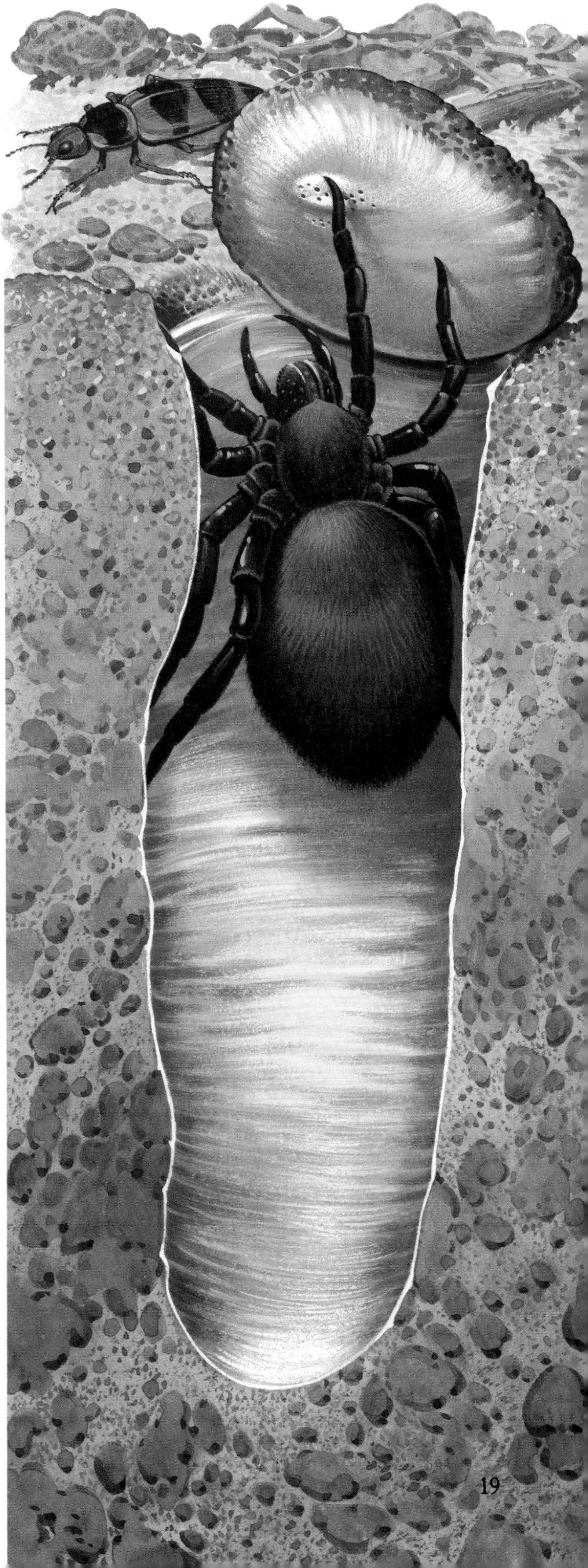

Woe betide the insect that ventures too near the roof of the Trapdoor spider's hide-out.

A column of Army ants may be 150,000 strong and can bring devastation to a jungle.

The Living Tank

Throughout South and Central America can be found a very peculiar group of mammals, the armadillos.

Every member of this group – there are about twenty species – is covered with strong bony plates. These plates provide a useful protection for the armadillos against attack. Only powerful predators would risk cracking their teeth on such a defence.

This bony armour marks the armadillos out from other mammals. No other mammal has such protection. Yet nobody is quite sure how this amazing defence system evolved. The skin of a mammal is covered with soft hairs and lacks the body plates frequently found in reptile skin, so there is no basic feature which could have evolved into the armadillos' armour. It is a feature unique to the armadillos.

However the plating may have evolved, it is basically the same throughout all the species of armadillo. First there is a solid shield over the shoulders of the animal and then another over its rump. Between the two are a series of bands, which may number between three and twenty. These bands allow for flexibility and permit the armadillo to adopt its basic defence posture. In the face of danger it will roll up into a ball, leaving few gaps in the armour for a predator to exploit. Alternatively, smaller species may attempt to burrow into the ground to ensure escape. The speed with which armadillos can react to the approach of a large animal has led some scientists to speculate that they are sensitive to ground vibrations which any large animal will make.

Being such a heavy animal it may be thought that an armadillo would have problems when it came to crossing water. This is not the case. Armadillos take

readily to water and have rarely been known to shirk a crossing. When faced with a stream that is shallow and not too wide, an armadillo will plunge in and scurry across the bed of the stream, allowing the water to flow over it. If, however, it must cross a more major river, an armadillo will literally swallow air until its stomach is fully extended. This acts as a kind of rubber ring, giving the creature extra bouyancy so that it can float.

Illustrated above are two of the strangest of the armadillos. First is the giant armadillo, a fifty kilo-gramme beast which is almost one and a half metres long. The giant armadillo is a powerful creature well able to rip open ants' nests with its strong front claws. It will then lap up the ants with its sticky tongue.

The much smaller fairy armadillo is a mere twelve centimetres long and has taken to an extreme the armadillo's burrowing abilities. This delicate creature

The Armadillos of South America are the only mammals to have evolved armour. In the illustration can be seen the Giant armadillo, left and the Fairy armadillo, right.

spends most of its life under the surface of the Argen-tinian plains in a series of burrows. It is thought to eat mainly roots and insects and has been compared with the mole in its lifestyle.

Any one of the armadillos is an oddity, but taken as a group they constitute one of the strangest mammalian families ever to walk the earth.

The Running Bird

Striding across the African plains at speeds approaching forty miles an hour, can be seen the largest bird in the world. It is the ostrich. This unmistakeable bird is the result of millions of years of evolution along a very peculiar road which led a family of birds to evolve to a life of flightlessness, and to acquire a number of special adaptations. In fact these adaptations are suited to a life running around on hot, arid plains which is just what the ostrich does.

Most noticeable of all are the drastic changes to wing and leg proportions. Unlike flying birds, the ostrich has wings which are tiny compared with its size and which are quite unable to support it in flight. The legs, on the other hand, are much better developed than in other birds. They are very long and are powered by strong muscles which are responsible for the bird's remarkable turn of speed.

In order to keep out the windblown dust and sand of the plains, the ostrich can close flaps of skin across its ears. It has also evolved long eyelashes to protect its eyes. However, it is the plumage of this bird which earned it a place in the world of fashion. The large, fluffy black and white feathers of the male were long used as hat decorations.

In the wild, ostriches are often found in the company of grazing zebras or gnus. This is a good example of two animals staying close to each other for mutual benefit. The grazing animals disturb seeds and insects for the ostriches to eat, while the tall ostriches keep a look out for predators.

The wings of the Ostrich are not powerful or big enough to enable it to fly like other birds.

The Tree Frog

The Tree frog may live in trees but it lays its eggs in water like other frogs.

Frogs are usually thought of as amphibians adapted to hopping around in damp meadows or near ponds but there is one group of frogs which do not conform at all. They are the tree frogs.

As the name implies, these strange amphibians are adapted to a life among the trees. They have very long hind legs with which they are able to leap from branch to branch. Compared with the ordinary frog, a tree frog is a phenomenal leaper. Not only can these frogs leap great distances, they can also leap very accurately. Indeed, many tree frogs hunt by leaping on to an insect from some distance away, snapping up the insect at the same moment that it lands.

Perhaps the biggest problem faced by a frog in a tree is what to do with its tadpoles. Most frogs lay their eggs in water, where they hatch into tadpoles and become frogs. As there is no water up a tree, most tree frogs solve this problem by simply climbing down and finding a convenient pond nearby. However the blacksmith frog is more ingenious. This species builds its own pond out of clay-like mud. When it rains, this artificial pond fills with water and is ready to receive the eggs. When the young frogs eventually develop, they return to the trees.

It may be thought that high in a tree is a rather precarious place for a small frog, but the tree frogs have another trick of nature up their sleeves. Each toe ends in an adhesive disc which can grip almost any surface. Indeed, a tree frog can grip easily to a pane of glass.

By a curious series of adaptations the tree frogs are, therefore, able to live in an environment which appears to be quite alien to them.

The Desert Racer

When the deserts of Arabia are mentioned the one animal which springs to mind is the camel. But there is another animal which is far more graceful than the camel and may be better adapted to desert life.

The oryx, seen below, is one of the most beautiful creatures in the world. Its lovely markings and horns pick it out from all the other species of antelope. Indeed, it has been suggested that the oryx is the inspiration behind the tales of the unicorn. Seen from the side, the Arabian oryx takes on the appearance of a small white horse with a single horn. It is not difficult to imagine travellers' tales exaggerating stories of this beautiful beast into the legend of the unicorn.

It is the remarkable powers of endurance of this beast, however, which make it of such interest to scientists. It is thought that the Arabian oryx can survive in temperatures of up to forty degrees centigrade and never need a drink of water. It appears that

24

the antelope gets all the water it needs from the desert plants on which it feeds.

Unfortunately, the Arabs have long believed that to kill a beautiful oryx is to prove one's worth as a hunter. Consequently, the oryx has been hunted to the verge of extinction. At one time there were only about fifty of these elegant creatures left but twenty years ago, conservationists began breeding the Arabian oryx in captivity. It now appears that the future of this most graceful of animals is assured.

The beautiful but very rare Arabian oryx is now a protected animal in the Arabian desert.

The Giant Anteater

The Giant anteater is strong enough to rip open a termite nest.

Roaming across the plains of South America is the awkward-looking creature seen above. It is a close relative of that other curiosity, the sloth, but it lives a quite different lifestyle. Indeed this lifestyle has given the creature its name, the giant anteater.

Though it may appear awkward and ungainly, this animal is ideally suited to its way of life. It has been estimated that the giant anteater needs around 30,000 ants or termites a day, so it has developed a very effective method of catching them.

First of all, it will find a termite nest, of which there are many on the sunbaked plains. Using its strong front claws, the anteater will then tear away at the nest until great gashes have been made in it. When the ants or termites come scurrying out to repair the damage, the anteater is waiting for them. Its long pointed snout

houses an equally long tongue, which is covered in sticky saliva. The anteater flicks this long tongue out, sweeping it to and fro, the ants become stuck to it and are then transferred to the mouth.

Though it is not an aggressive animal, the anteater is well able to look after itself if attacked. It will rear up on its hind legs and lash out with its powerful and sharp claws. This display, from a beast almost three metres long, is enough to deter even the most ferocious of predators.

This gentle giant belongs to a type of mammal known as edentates, which also includes the armadillos seen on page 20. Scientists have found fossils which show that edentates first evolved more than fifty million years ago.

Hidden Weapons

Birds are always on the lookout for a tasty morsel and juicy caterpillars are high on their list. When, though, a bird is foolhardy enough to tackle the puss-moth caterpillar, it is in for a nasty shock.

This small, seemingly helpless, insect does, in fact, have a complicated and effective defence. To start with, it is very well camouflaged in shades of green and brown, so most of the time it escapes being seen. However, when a bird closes in for the attack, the caterpillar will raise its body up and wave its whip-like prolegs in a threatening manner. If this fails to deter the attacker, the caterpillar squirts a stream of formic acid at the aggressor. This sudden and unexpected attack is enough to put off most hunters and ensures safety for the caterpillar.

Birds fancying to make a meal out of a Puss-moth caterpillar are in for a nasty surprise.

The small Spitting cobra repels danger by ejecting a stream of unpleasant liquid.

Long Range Venom

In India and Africa there lives a family of poisonous snakes known as the cobras. These snakes share many characteristics, of which the most noticeable is the hood behind the head. This extends when the snake is about to strike, giving it a most sinister appearance.

At five metres in length, the king cobra of India is the largest snake. But perhaps the strangest is the much smaller spitting cobra which squirts its venom out of its mouth. The jet of venom can reach a range of several metres. It is rarely accurate at more than two metres. If the venom gets into another creature's eyes, it can cause temporary blindness, giving the spitting snake time to escape. This peculiar ability is due to the fact that the poison channels in the fangs bend at right angles and emerge through holes at the front of the fangs, rather than at the back as is more usual.

27

The Master Builder

The creature with perhaps the most amazing construction abilities in the animal world is the beaver. This large furry rodent is able to fell trees, dam rivers and build ingenious houses in which it lives.

There are, in fact, two species of beaver, the European and the North American, but they are very similar to each other. The short, thick-set body on four strong, sturdy legs is crowned by a broad head set on a flexible neck. The beaver shows many adaptations to a life in the water, where adult beavers spend most of their time. The hind legs of the beaver have webbed feet, which enables it to swim faster, and the tail is thickened into a broad paddle-like organ which is used as a rudder when the beaver is swimming. The

beaver is also able to close its nostrils to prevent water from entering.

It is the building ability of the beaver which really picks it out from other large rodents. Using only the simplest of materials, branches, stones and mud, the beaver can construct a dam across a river, creating an artificial lake.

The dams are built in the summer, when there is plenty of water and wood available and the weather is fine. Using their strong front teeth, the beavers gnaw through the trunks of trees, bringing them crashing to the ground. The tree is then stripped of its branches, which are dragged by the beaver to the site of the dam. Here they are piled together to form a complex, intertwining pattern of great strength. After being weighted down with stones the dam is then plastered

with a mixture of mud and leaves to further water-proof it. Should a section of dam become damaged, the beavers quickly respond to the sound of escaping water and patch up the gap. These dams can be very large. One was once measured and found to be five hundred metres long and four metres high.

In the still, sheltered water behind the dam, the beavers construct their lodges. These are built in a similar way to the dam, being made up of sticks, stones and mud. All beaver lodges follow a roughly similar plan, though they may be any size up to five metres across.

In the centre is a large room in which the beaver family lives and stores food, bark and twigs, for the winter. From this chamber two tunnels exit and emerge under the water of the lake. One is broad and

Beavers are among the master builders of the animal world and are able to build dams and lodges.

slopes gently. This is used for bringing in food. The other is narrow and steep and is generally used by the beavers for entering and leaving the lodge.

Inside this cunningly-built lodge, the beavers keep warm during the long cold winter and here they have a constant supply of food. They are also safe from attack, as animals which prey on the beaver cannot swim and the entrance to the lodge is under water.

All the effort of building and maintaining dams and lodges during the summer gives security in the winter for the beaver, the master builder of nature.

The Ship Destroyer

Living in the warm waters of the world's oceans is a small, harmless looking creature just a few centimetres in length. Yet this small animal has been the cause of more danger and worry for sailors in the past than perhaps any other. It is the shipworm.

The shipworm will settle on any waterlogged timbers as a tiny larva, and start to burrow into the wood, leaving a tiny pinprick of a hole. As it tunnels through, digesting the wood as it goes, the worm increases in size until it is about sixty centimetres long. In a surprisingly short period of time, perhaps as little as six months, the tunnelling of shipworms will reduce a piece of wood to a fragile shell. The only sign on the outside of the timber, if examined, will be a number of tiny holes which could quite easily go unnoticed.

In the early days of seafaring, there can be no doubt

Before a method of controlling it was discovered, the Shipworm (inset) probably caused many shipwrecks.

that numerous ships sank and many lives were lost because important timbers were weakened and gave way as a result of tunnelling shipworms. However, once sailors knew that shipworms were the problem, they could find ways to defeat them. At first ships' hulls were covered with tar and other noxious substances to stop the worms settling in the first place. This solution helped, but did not stop shipworms altogether. The final solution was not found until the eighteenth century when ships were sheathed with copper plates.

Today, in the days of metal ships, the shipworm is not such a problem, but it still remains the smallest animal able to sink a ship.

The Fish that Flies

The first sailors to see fish belonging to the family Exocoetoidae must have thought they were dreaming, and their tales were dismissed as tall stories. This is because the fishes of this family appear to fly through the air.

It is true that these fishes suddenly leap from the sparkling water and cover tremendous distances before splashing back into the sea. But it is not true that they fly. What these creatures are actually doing is gliding. It is thought that this strange behaviour may be a defence mechanism. After all, a fish suddenly taking off from the water would be enough to confuse any predator.

Before take off, this thirty centimetre long fish will swim along just below the surface of the sea at tremendous speed, sometimes as much as fifty kilometres an hour. With a sudden flick of its tail, which may be beating many times each second, the fish leaps from the water. It is at this point that its special adaptations come into their own. The pectoral fins are greatly enlarged, out of all proportion to the size of the fish. As soon as it is airborne, the fish spreads these fins out to form 'wings' with which it can glide. Some of the leaps or glides performed by flying fishes are truly remarkable. One glide lasted for several seconds and covered a full three hundred metres, making this the only fish that is at home in the air as much as it is in the water.

The Flying fish does not in fact fly. It glides.

31

The Inflatable Fish

Swimming off the Atlantic Coast of North America is a small fish which at first glance appears defenceless. The porcupine fish, as it is known, has an extremely effective method of self defence and one which is very unusual.

When faced with attack, this small fish will start taking great gulps of water. This causes the body of the porcupine fish to swell up to enormous proportions. This sudden increase in size would probably be enough to put off most predators, but the porcupine fish is also armed with numerous spines which become erect as the body swells. All in all it is a difficult fish to catch.

The odd-looking fish below has spines similar in appearance to those of a porcupine. Hence its name of Porcupine fish. When danger threatens it inflates its body, and the spines are erect giving the fish all round protection.

A Fish on Dry Land

Perhaps the most extraordinary fish of all is the small fish pictured above, the mudskipper.

This fish is very rare in that it is as much at home on land as it is in the water. It lives along the shores of the Indian Ocean and in brackish mangrove swamps and rivers. Much of the time it lives as any other fish does, swimming around in the water looking for food. Often the search for food, in this case insects, leads the mudskipper on to land.

As their name suggests, these fish spend their time out of water mainly on mud flats. They move by using their muscular pectoral fins, those nearest the head, to push themselves along. It has even been known for the mudskipper to climb mangrove trees in the search for food.

Of course, the greatest problem facing the mudskipper is how to breathe. In the water it uses its gills to remove the oxygen dissolved in water and it has no lungs to breathe air. It manages to get round this

The Dangerous Dragonfish

Cruising the waters of the Indian Ocean is the thirty centimetre long dragonfish pictured below. Despite its size, this fish is quite safe from attack by predators, due to a remarkable adaptation which it has evolved.

Each of the long delicate spines protruding from its body is loaded with poison. The spines can cause a very painful wound which deters any attacker. The distinctive markings of the fish are easily recognisable and warn a predator that the dragonfish is dangerous to tackle. The predator generally takes the warning and leaves the dragonfish in peace.

The poisoned spines are, in fact, modified fins which have evolved over millions of years into their present form, relegating their use as fins to second place.

The appearance of a Dragonfish is enough to daunt a would-be attacker.

When on land the mudskipper blends in well with its surroundings and is therefore protected.

problem by filling special sacs with water and then using this water to moisten its gills. This is not a particularly effective method of breathing and the mudskipper must return to the sea to refill its sacs fairly often, but it has enabled the mudskipper to colonise the land.

Many millions of years ago another fish was dragging itself across the mud with its fins. Scientists have named this fish *Eusthenopteron* and belonged to a group of fish known as the lobe-finned fish. At that time there were no mammals or reptiles living on the land. Lobe-finned fish were the only vertebrates to move on dry land. The fins of the *Eusthenopteron* had a strong bony core. In time strong fins developed and evolved until they became legs. The lobe-finned fishes were the ancestors of all land based vertebrates. The little mudskipper gives us an idea of how lobe-fins lived.

The Coral Polyp

Running for many hundreds of miles off the east coast of Australia is the Great Barrier Reef, which lies just below the sea surface and has caused the wrecking of more than one ship. There are hundreds of similar reefs throughout the Pacific Ocean.

The corals, which can be of many beautiful shapes and sizes, are the accumulated skeletons of thousands upon thousands of tiny animals known as coral polyps. Each polyp is no larger than a pin, so the way they manage to build such huge reefs is very interesting.

The coral polyps themselves are soft bodied creatures, related to jellyfish. They live by filtering food from the sea water and they need a secure base on which to attach themselves. Each coral polyp secretes a calcereous material, known as aragonite, which is as hard as rock. It forms this into a cup-shaped structure and attaches itself to the base of the cup. Whenever danger threatens, the polyp can withdraw into its cup.

Obviously a stony cup the size of a pinhead is not going to become a mighty reef. The secret of the reefs is the fact that coral polyps like living together. As the thousands upon thousands of polyp cups are built next to each other and on top of each other, a sizeable mound is created. It is this accumulation of polyp

skeletons in great numbers in one place which forms a reef.

It is generally agreed that there are hundreds of species of polyp but only three types of reef. These are the fringing reef, the barrier reef and the atoll.

Corals need shallow water and warm temperatures to thrive and for this reason are often found along the shores of tropical islands. A fringing reef is a reef growing around an island. A barrier reef, on the other hand, grows some way out from the land, creating a shallow lagoon. This type of reef usually occurs when an island is sinking, leaving the coral stranded far from its shores.

How then to explain an atoll, a ring of coral with no island in the centre? Atolls are simply barrier reefs which have progressed further. The island has sunk completely, leaving only the ring of coral which once surrounded it.

But whatever type of polyp or coral composes it, a reef is an important ecological environment, providing a home for many different animals and plants.

The many varied and beautiful coral reefs are formed by the action of tiny animals called Coral polyps.

35

The Submerged Spider

We all know that spiders spin webs, but few know that not all webs catch insects. There is one species of spider which has adapted its web to a quite different purpose.

The water spider builds a web in the shape of a dome and attaches it to the stalk of a water plant a few centimetres below the surface. This dome is then patiently filled with air by the spider. Each time the spider visits the surface, air becomes trapped by hairs on its body. When it reaches the nest, the spider rubs itself to release the air. In this way the web becomes a kind of airtight bell for the spider.

Within the web the spider lives and lays its eggs. When these hatch, the tiny young hurry out of the nest and head for the surface to get their first taste of fresh air. In time they will also construct their own underwater nests, continuing the cycle.

The food of the water spider consists mainly of water insects. When it leaves the nest to hunt, the water spider traps air around its body to last until its return. Despite its aquatic lifestyle, the water spider has not yet mastered eating under water. It must therefore return to the air bubble of its nest to consume its prey.

Though spiders are sometimes confused with insects they do, in fact, belong to a quite different class of invertebrates, the arachnids. One of the main distinguishing features of the arachnids is the fact that they have eight legs, rather than the six of the insects.

The water spider does not use its web to trap food but actively hunts. The great bird-eating spider is also an active hunter. It will usually hide itself in a burrow, sometimes lined with silk, until a likely bird or small mammal comes by. The spider will then leap out and try to bite the prey with its poisoned fangs. If it is successful and the prey is paralysed the spider will eat its victim at leisure.

The Water spider weaves a web like other species of spiders but uses it differently.

An Expert Shot

Visually the archer fish of South East Asia is not particularly interesting. It is a small fish, about 18 centimetres long, coloured silver with a number of bars down its flanks. But its method of catching food is spectacular and possibly unique.

The archer fish cruises along just under the surface of the lake or river until it sees an insect resting on a branch overhanging the river. The fish will then carefully position itself and push its snout up out of the water. Suddenly it shoots a powerful jet of water from its mouth with remarkable precision. Usually this hits the insect, knocking it into the water where the fish eats it.

The jet of water is produced by special adaptations to the fish's mouth. The tongue is muscular and has a groove running along it. When the fish wishes to shoot down an insect it takes a mouthful of water and squirts it out by forcing the tongue on to the roof of the mouth. The strength of the tongue directs the water along the groove until it emerges as the powerful jet.

Archer fish are able to send a stream of water over distances of a metre and still hit a target the size of a fly.

Such an ability to catch insects out of the water, as well as in it, is a great advantage to this small fish. The archer fish seems assured of a long and prosperous future.

The Archer fish attacks the insects it eats by accurately shooting them down with a jet of water.

Undersea Dangers?

In the waters of the Pacific Ocean lives a creature which has figured in many lurid tales of the sea, the giant clam. This animal is usually pictured holding on to a diver's foot and gripping him in a deadly embrace.

But the truth is rather more mundane. If a giant clam did take hold of a diver it would be purely by chance. The giant clam, like most bivalves, lives by filtering food from the sea water. Bivalves are shellfish with two shells. By opening and closing its shells rhythmically, the giant clam draws water through a special filter around the edges of the shells. This filter traps tiny microscopic plants which float around in the seas.

It is its size that makes the giant clam so different from other bivalves.

It is one and a half metres across and is the largest bivalve that has ever evolved. Compared to the six centimetre mussel or the three centimetre clam, the giant clam is truly astounding. Because of its great bulk, it is unable to swim, as do other bivalves. Instead the giant clam is firmly anchored to the sea floor by a muscular foot which keeps a firm grip on rocks. Among its favourite locations are coral reefs (see page 35) where it can find an abundance of food.

Living in the Pacific Ocean alongside the giant clam is the sailfish, which may also be seen in the illustration below. It is quite clear from its appearance why this fish is so named.

The 'sail' on its back is, in reality, a dorsal fin such as any fish may have. The extraordinarily long spines of this fin are very stiff and support a flap of skin, creating the sail effect. No one is quite sure what purpose the sail fulfils, but it may help to stabilise the fish when it is swimming.

The other obvious feature of the fish is its elongated upper jaw. This feature is shared by the swordfish, to

38

which the sailfish is related. Again nobody can say definitely for what the 'sword' is used.

There is one thing which can be stated for certain about this large sea fish. It is a much coveted game fish. Private yachts put out to sea, full of elaborate fishing tackle which the occupants hope will help them catch a large sailfish. Really big sailfish may be four metres long and weigh well over one hundred kilograms.

If the fisherman succeeds in hooking a sailfish, he is faced with a long and exciting fight which he may well lose. The sailfish is an expert at escaping the hook. It will leap into the air, as shown on page 4, or speed through the water until it is exhausted or it is free.

Though the Giant clam is no danger to divers, the Sailfish, below and on page 4, is a tough catch for anglers.

Swimming Birds

In the southern hemisphere lives a family of birds quite unlike any other which is adapted to a life in the seas. The penguins' bright coats, awkward gait and lively antics are familiar to many, but their true environment is the water.

Once in the water, penguins become creatures of great grace and beauty. Their lithe, torpedo-shaped bodies are ideal for swimming, gliding through the water, generating little resistance. The short, broad wings which make flight impossible, also come into their own underwater. The wings are superb flippers which power the bird through the water at great speed. They work in much the same way as do the wings of normal birds in flight. So it might be said that penguins 'fly' through the water. While the wings power the bird through the water, its short and ungainly legs steer it. The toes of the penguin are

(continued on page 40)

39

webbed and are very strong, enabling the bird to change direction quickly. The penguin's speed and manoevrability enable it to be an excellent swimmer and to catch its main food, fish.

When in search of this food, penguins have been known to spend months at sea and to cover vast distances. But they must return to land once a year to lay eggs and to rear their young.

Of all the penguins, the emperor penguin has perhaps the most amazing breeding cycle. The emperors come ashore in the autumn in flocks numbering thousands. After congregating at recognised breeding grounds, the females lay their eggs and head back to the sea. The eggs are taken over by the males, who look after them for the next two

Among the many species of penguin that inhabit the South Pole are the Emperor, left, the Jackass, above left and the Rock Hopper.

months. During this time, the males huddle together for warmth and keep the egg protected against the winter temperatures of forty below freezing.

When the chick hatches, the female returns and takes over care of the young, while the male takes to the water in search of food. By the summer months the chick is old enough to catch its own fish, and takes to the sea.

Though a rather primitive group, there are many species of penguin, each very different. They are scattered across half the globe which would indicate success, and yet their shared characteristics, such as a composite bill, would seem to point to penguins not being as advanced as other birds. Indeed, fossils over thirty million years old reveal that the ancient

penguins were not much different from modern ones.

These birds, which can be both awkward and graceful and can survive in the inhospitable Antarctic wastes, are truly remarkable creatures. They are adapted to a life in the water to an extent unknown to other birds and have managed to win the hearts of countless sailors by their amusing antics.

The Hunter of the Deep

Thousands of feet below the surface of the sea is a strange and little known world. No light can penetrate from above and the water is an unrelieved inky blackness. The massive weight of water pushing down means that the pressure is many times greater than that which would crush the bodies of most living things. Any creature which manages to survive in such an inhospitable environment must be a very remarkable animal.

One such creature is the sinister-looking fish pictured below, the deep sea angler. Specially adapted to survive the terrible pressures of the ocean depths, this creature hunts the cold, still waters throughout its life.

Food, in such an environment, is hard to come by and the angler must be sure to catch any which comes its way.

The light which dangles on a 'rod' above its head gives the angler its name. It is with this bait that it traps its prey. Most fish are attracted to light, and any fish which lives in blackness is even more strongly drawn. But when a fish comes to investigate the waiting deep sea angler's lure, it finds the ferocious jaws and needle-sharp teeth waiting to seize and crush it.

It is not only the light which marks the angler out from other fish. Its breeding habits are also unusual. The male fastens itself on to the side of the female and lives as a parasite for the rest of its life, living off the blood of its mate.

In our picture, you can see the tiny male attached to the side of the female.

The deep sea Angler fish hunts other fish with the aid of its light.

The Eastern Fighter

The Siamese fighting fish, fights its own kind in spectacular bouts.

Living in the rivers of the Far East is a freshwater relative of the flying fish, the Siamese fighting fish. Though only a few inches long, the males of this fish are well known as fearsome battlers.

In the wild, encounters occur relatively rarely and are quickly over. But in the Eastern country of Thailand, the wild fish have been selectively bred for thousands of years to produce a fish capable of truly remarkable battles. When two males are placed in an aquarium together, they will instantly attack each other. They seize each other by their mouths and wrestle, flinging themselves around in the water, turning this way and that, until one of them is finally exhausted and gives up. As can been seen, the fish are not only bred for their fighting abilities, but also for their looks. They are perhaps the most beautiful gladiators ever to fight for the amusement of others.

The fish breeders of the Orient have also turned their skills to breeding fish solely for their looks. The well known goldfish is a product of the same breeding techniques.

When it comes to laying eggs, the fighting fish employ a method known as bubble nest building. The male will blow bubbles near the surface of the water, using a special mucus, which he secretes. Once a suitable raft of bubbles has been constructed, the female will lay her eggs upon it. It is then up to the male to look after the eggs until they have hatched. But once the young fish have hatched, they have to be careful for their parents will more than likely try to eat them.

The Long-legged Crab

There are various species of Spider crab and they live in many of the seas.

As a group, crabs must be among the most unusual creatures in the seas. They belong to the same group of crustaceans as shrimps and lobsters, but are distinguished by their shells. The upper shell of a crab covers its entire body, while its underside is protected by the hard tail which is permanently bent under the body.

There are many species of crab, running into thousands. The one with the oddest appearance must surely be the Japanese spider crab, shown above. Spider crabs have legs which are very long and thin in relation to the rest of their bodies. Of the six hundred odd species of spider crab, the Japanese is the largest.

A large male may measure a good three metres across the spread of its legs, though the body itself is not much larger than that of other large crabs. The spider crab finds its way across the sea floor in much the same way as other crabs, with a curious sideways scuttle of surprising speed.

It hunts its food with its large and powerful pincers, which it uses to grab any small animals that come within reach. The sharp claws will then crush the life from the victim before it is eaten.

In common with most other spider crabs, the Japanese species will often cover itself with seaweed to ensure being camouflaged and so escape any hungry predators.

The waters off Japan hold another curious crab. The shell of one species has a pattern that resembles the frown and helmet of a samurai warrior. Because of Japanese superstition the fishermen will throw any of these crabs back, so the species continues to prosper.

The Mouth-brooder

Fish can lay their eggs in some very odd places. We have seen that the Siamese fighting fish will lay its eggs on a raft of air bubbles, but by far the most unusual shelter for eggs has been found by the African mouth-brooder, a type of cichlid. It keeps its eggs in its mouth.

When the time comes to spawn, the male will dig a shallow hole in the sand or mud. Into this the female will lay her eggs and then instantly turn round and gobble them up. But she does not eat them. Instead she keeps the tiny eggs in her mouth, safe from any other fish which might try to devour them. After about a week, the eggs hatch out and perfectly formed young swim out of their mother's mouth. But this is not the end of the story. Even after the young have hatched and are swimming on their own, they may nip back into their mother's mouth if any danger threatens.

It must be one of the most unusual sights in the world to see one fish swim quite willingly into the mouth of the other.

The mouth-brooder is not the only cichlid fish to indulge in unusual breeding habits. Other species of the group will lay their eggs in a shallow nest and will then guard them against all intruders. This protective instinct, which is common among land animals but strangely quite unusual amongst fish, can often prove dangerous for the parents, as they are willing to battle predators many times their own size to protect the eggs.

The Mouth-brooder shown here is not eating. It is allowing its young to take shelter in its mouth.

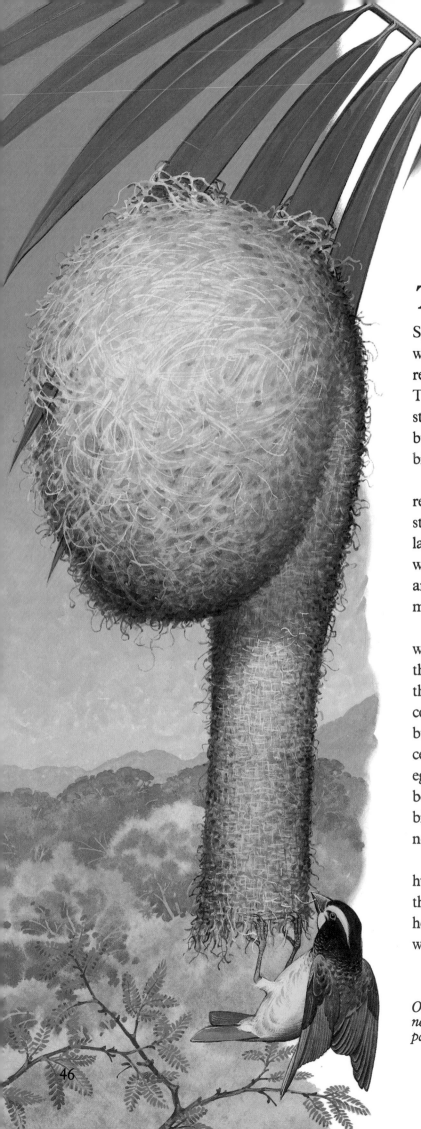

The Avian Architect

Spread across Africa, and most of the rest of the world, is a group of birds which build the most remarkable nests. They are known as weaver-birds. Thought to have originated in Africa, where they are still very prolific, the various members of this group build the most intricate nests of any constructed by birds.

A single glance at the nest pictured on the left will reveal why the birds are so named. Hundreds of strands of grass have been woven together to form a large and cunningly designed nest. The weaver bird will collect grass and twigs together from a wide area and then, using only its beak, it will weave the materials together into a nest.

The various species of weaver-bird have different ways of building. In some species the male will do all the construction work, whilst in others it is the work of the female. The shape of the nest can also vary quite considerably. The nest illustrated here is of the type built by the Baya weaver-bird of south-east Asia. The central bulge is the location of the actual nest, where eggs are laid and chicks brought up. The tube hanging below this is, in fact, a narrow tunnel. This is only just big enough for a weaver-bird to enter and its narrowness keeps out any large predators.

Some weaver-birds build their nests together in huge colonies. These communal nests look like thatched roofs hanging in trees and are sometimes so heavy that a tree will crash to the ground under their weight.

One of the many species of Weaver bird and its nest is shown here. Each species constructs its own particular shaped nest.

The Useful Insect

Many insects are harmful to man, either because they carry disease or because they destroy crops. But the well-known honey bee, above, is of great benefit to man.

Honey bees live in large colonies, sometimes many thousands strong, which work on a highly organised system. There are three basic types of bee in each colony: the queen, the worker and the drone.

The queen, as her name suggests, is the most important member of the colony. She lays eggs and so ensures the survival of the swarm, but she could not survive on her own.

The workers, again according to their name, are the members of the hive which perform most of the activities necessary for the swarm's survival. It is the workers who build the comb out of wax and who constantly repair it. They also fly out in search of the nectar and pollen on which the hive feeds.

The well-known Honey bee collects pollen and nectar which are then made into honey.

It is this aspect of the bee's life history which is useful to man. The nectar collected from flowers is made into honey, a popular product used in many kitchens. But of far more financial importance to man is the fact that bees are responsible for pollinating many crops in field or orchard. Without this important service, many crops such as apples and pears would not develop.

In contrast to the queen and the workers, the drones, or males, do not seem to do much at all. When the queen sets off to found a new hive, the drones fly with her to fertilise the eggs, but otherwise perform no work and only live a few months.

Birds from Paradise

In 1522 Magellan's ship, the *Victoria*, returned to Spain after completing the very first circumnavigation of the world. Amongst the many travellers' tales and exotic goods the crew had picked up on their epic voyage were the feathered skins of two birds. These had been a gift from the ruler of Bajan to the King of Spain. When they were shown at court, because the feathers were so beautiful and ornate, nobody would believe that they were from ordinary birds at all. Instead it was thought that they had come from Paradise.

Today we know that the birds live on New Guinea and several nearby islands. However, the name bird of

paradise has stuck and it is by this nomenclature that they are still known. It is not difficult to see how the name became so popular, for the many species of bird all have the most wonderful plumage.

This beautiful display of feathers has a purpose. It is the males who have the beautiful colours and outlandish displays. The females are, on the whole, rather drab birds, coloured a dismal brown. This helps them to hide amid the jungle foliage and to escape the attacks of predators.

The males, however, do not wish to hide. On the contrary, they wish to advertise their presence. In the gloomy rain forest jungles in which they live, this is no easy task. The brilliant displays they put on help them to be seen and to attract the females. The bewildering

Above are a few of the magnificent birds of paradise. From left to right they are; the Superb, the Magnificent rifle, the Little King, Prince Rudolph's blue bird, the Greater, and above it, the King of Saxony. More of these birds can be seen on pages 6 and 7.

variety of form and colour is simply a means of telling the female to which species the male belongs. If it were not for their plumage, the various species would appear very much alike.

About a hundred years ago, the feathers, which for centuries had guaranteed the survival of birds of paradise, almost led to their extinction. In the latter part of the nineteenth century, it was fashionable in Europe for ladies to wear feathers in their hats. The more colourful the feather, the more fashionable the hat. As a result the feathers of the birds of paradise were much sought after and thousands of birds were captured and killed.

Luckily this trade in feathers no longer exists, but it is surprising how little is known about the life and habits of these glorious birds. Because they live in the depths of some of the densest jungle in the world, very few scientists have been able to study them. In fact some species of bird of paradise are only known from one or two skins brought out of the jungle by native tribesmen.

Flying Mammals

The only order of mammals which has successfully taken to the air is the Chiroptera, the bats. Though usually thought of as repulsive and frightening creatures of the night, they are, in fact, a very interesting group of creatures. Some of them are active during the day.

It is known that the bats are one of the oldest forms of mammal. The earliest fossils date back some fifty million years to the Eocene era. Known to the present day scientists as *Icaronycteris*, this ancient bat was as perfectly adapted for a life in the air as modern bats are.

The existence of such an advanced animal would indicate that even at that remote stage of history, the bats were an old order.

Bats in general can fly as well as birds. But the means by which they fly are quite different. The wings of a bird are constructed of feathers which overlap each other and are attached to the bird's forelimb. The bat has no feathers, so its forelimb must form the wing itself. The fingers of the bat's arm are incredibly lengthened and a flap of skin stretches between the fingers and the body. This flap of leathery skin forms the wing and is a very efficient flying mechanism.

However, bats have had to pay a high price for their ability to fly. The large area of skin means that a lot of water is lost through evaporation. As the wing is

Bats are the only mammals to take to the air successfully. Among them are the flower-faced below.

50

The Flying fox above and on the end-papers is a fruit-eating animal.

supplied with many blood vessels, much heat is lost as well. Taken together, these factors mean that the bat loses a lot of heat and water which must be constantly replenished. This dual need accounts for the voracious appetites of the bats. They have to eat almost continuously to survive.

There are two main groups of bat, the fruit bats and the insectivorous bats. The fruit bats are the larger of the two and seek out fruit trees for their food. The flying fox from India, which is pictured above, can measure almost two metres from wingtip to wingtip. These large bats roost in large colonies in trees during the day and emerge at dusk for their daily feast.

The insectivorous bats are the more well-known.

The flower-faced bat, pictured on the left, belongs to this group. These much smaller bats, some only a few inches across, hunt insects on the wing. To locate the fast flying insects, these bats have evolved a type of natural sonar. The bat emits a very short, high pitched noise which echoes back off any object. From the type of echo it receives, the bat can make out what the object is and how fast it is moving. This means the bat is able to capture many a juicy morsel.

The grotesque flaps of skin found on the faces of so many of these bats are simply aids to the emission of the ultrasonic sounds.

There can be little doubt that this ancient group is one of the oddest orders of mammal in the world.

The Gardening Bird

Birds will go to great lengths to attract a mate. On page 48 you can see the glorious plumage of the male birds of paradise. But no bird works harder than the bowerbird.

There are some eighteen species of bowerbird spread around Australia and New Guinea and most of them build bowers of one kind or another.

Perhaps the most impressive of the bowers is that built by the orange crested gardener bird of New Guinea. This small bird, only 20 centimetres long, together with some other species, builds a 'maypole' type of bower. First the bird will find two small trees or shrubs a few feet apart in a patch of open ground. Having cleared the ground of any dead leaves or other debris, the bird starts to build.

It piles sticks and bits of wood around the base of one of the trees until the pile is about six feet tall. A similar pile is then built around the other tree and the two connected with a thatched roof of sticks and leaves. Once the main construction work of the bower itself is completed, the bird decorates it. Bright berries and flowers are collected and spread about the bower,

The orange crested bower bird decorates its home with flowers and berries.

and are replaced immediately they fade and die.

It also plants mosses in the area in front of the bower, which continue to grow for some time.

These bowers may be used year after year, being repaired and added to continuously. It is this continuity which makes the gardener bird unique among bowerbirds.

All the time and effort spent on the bowers by the male bowerbirds is an effort to attract female birds. It is not used as a nest at all. The eggs are laid in a much smaller, rather ordinary nest. It would seem that, like the plumage of the birds of paradise, the bowers are a means of being seen and recognised in the dark jungle.

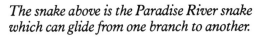

The snake above is the Paradise River snake which can glide from one branch to another.

The Flying Snake

Many snakes are adapted for a life in the trees, being able to climb and hunt very well in the branches. One of these snakes has the ability to glide from one branch to another. It does this by pulling in the scales along its underside to form a concave shape, which increases air resistance. As a result the snake is able to descend far more slowly than would otherwise be the case and therefore make a safe landing.

It is said that the snake uses this ability of gliding slowly, to land on and surprise the birds on which it feeds. But it may be instead the case that the snake glides to escape predators. Whatever the truth of the matter, this snake remains the only one which can 'fly'.

53

The Stink Bird

The Hoatzin of South America is an ungainly bird which has an unpleasant smell.

Living in the thick Amazonian jungles of South America is the curious bird shown above. It is known as the hoatzin, but it has such a strong and unusual smell that locals call it the stink bird.

This bird shows many characteristics not found in other birds. Indeed, scientists are still not sure in which group to place it nor where it fits into the evolutionary story of the birds.

This twenty-five centimetre long bird lives in bushes and trees along the banks of streams and rivers. Along these banks, it searches for its main food, the leaves of the arum plant. Because of an incredibly large crop, which runs down the front of the bird, the hoatzin has very weak wing muscles. As a result it is such a poor flier that it can barely manage to glide from one side of the stream to the other.

However, it is a feature of the young chicks which is of the greatest interest to scientists. On the front of their wings, the chicks have sharp claws. They use these claws to climb around in the branches of the shrubs in which they live. These claws are not found in any other living bird and may be an indication of the reptilian ancestry of the hoatzin.

The Insect Eaters

The nightjars are one of the most widespread type of all the birds. There are some sixty-seven species spread across every continent in the world. Only New Zealand seems free of them. Their range across the rest of the world is only limited by the availability of food. Since this food is insects they can live almost everywhere.

Two African species of nightjar flaunt some very unusual courting feathers.

During the spring, the innermost wing feathers of the male pennant-wing nightjar grow to the amazing length of seventy centimetres, over twice the length of the bird itself.

When in flight, the male will circle the female, making sweeping, soaring patterns in the sky. These antics show off the long wing feathers to best advantage.

It seems that this unusual display takes the place of the calls of other nightjars, for the pennant-wing is totally voiceless. Another African species with similar plumage is the standard-wing nightjar. This has similarly long wing feathers, but in this case, the feathers are bare for most of their length, only having vanes for the last few inches.

In common with all other nightjars, these two species are mainly nocturnal and are therefore dull in colour. But during the day, when the nightjar is resting, its drab colouring renders it almost invisible against the background of dead leaves or bark, where it lurks.

In fact, the nightjar is so confident of its effective camouflage that it will not move until it is almost trodden upon. Then it moves – and fast!

Many species of Nightjar can be seen all over the world excepting New Zealand.

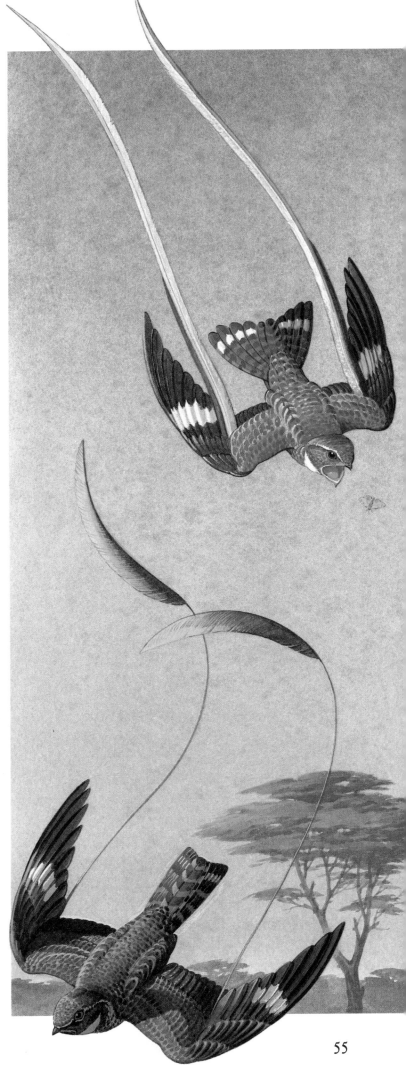

55

The Masters of Flight

It is generally recognised that birds are supreme in the air and there can be little doubt that the most skilful amongst them are the hummingbirds. These birds can fly up, down, sideways, forwards and backwards. Their flight of quick bursts and sudden stops is bewildering, especially as their wings beat too quickly for the human eye to see.

This remarkable flying ability is due to a number of factors. First these beautifully coloured birds are tiny. This small size gives a high ratio between wing surface and weight, making unusual flying antics possible. About a quarter of the weight of any hummingbird is taken up by its wing muscles, which are incredibly powerful. These strong muscles can beat the bird's wings at speeds of two hundred strokes a second. It is the rapid movement of the wings through the air which produces the distinctive humming sound for which the birds are known. By way of contrast, the voices of hummingbirds are not impressive – few can manage more than a thin squeak.

The full speed of two hundred wing beats a second is only used during courtship. Normal flight requires about half that rate, while hovering demands around sixty beats a second. The amount of energy burned up by the birds during this incredible flying means that they need a food which yields a high level of calories.

The highest calorie food is sugar and this is found in abundance in nectar. Nectar is a strong sugary solution produced by flowers at the base of their petals. It attracts insects to cross-pollinate the flowers. The beaks of the hummingbirds are ideally suited to sucking out the nectar of flowers. In most species the beaks are long and thin, often slightly curved, for reaching into the very depths of the blooms. The birds have not only the advantage of long beaks, but their tongues are made to extend beyond the beak to lap or suck up every available drop of nectar. Some hummingbirds have very weirdly shaped bills. The swordbilled hummingbird of the Andes, for example, has a long straight bill some twelve centimetres long.

Hummingbirds are the best fliers in the world of birds. Those here from left to right are the Ruby topaz (male) Sword bill, the Ruby topaz (female), the Sickle bill, the Andean emerald, the Blue-throated sylph, the Velvet purple coronet and the Rufous tailed.

This beak is longer than the rest of the bird; body, head and tail put together. At the other extreme, the white-tipped sicklebill has a short beak, but one which is bent round almost into a semicircle.

These delightful and colourful inhabitants of the New World are surely the most skilled masters of flight.

The Paper Wasp

When a queen wasp of the species *Polistes annularis* wakes up from her winter hibernation she starts to look for a nesting spot. This is usually in some protected place, often in a garden shed or other building. Having found a spot, she will start to build.

It is at this point that she earns her popular name, the paper wasp. She starts by chewing up tiny pieces of wood until they form a pulp. Then, using her saliva, she will attach a lump of the pulp to a secure place. Using this as a stalk, the wasp then expands the nest until it is large enough to hold eggs.

The concoction of wood pulp and saliva dries out to form a substance which is very like paper. The nest is therefore very light and can be repaired easily.

The first batch of eggs are raised by the queen herself. These eggs hatch into worker wasps, which then take over the running of the nest. The queen lays more and more eggs and the larvae must be fed. This is done by the workers. Each time the workers bring a larva a meal, the larva secretes a sweet substance that the workers like to eat. In this way they are encouraged to continue feeding the larvae.

At the end of each summer a few new queens are hatched. These fly off to find somewhere to hibernate for the winter. So the cycle is completed. It can therefore be seen that the wasp is not only a clever builder, but also a creature with a well developed social life.

The bold yellow and black markings of the wasp may seem out of place when most insects try to avoid being seen by predators. But the very boldness is a form of protection. Birds soon learn that a wasp has a nasty sting. If the wasp is able to inform other creatures that it is an insect with a sting, they will leave it alone. The bright markings do just that.

The queen Paper wasp builds this delicate nest and then lays her first batch of eggs.

58

Locusts dispose of hundreds of square miles of crops and vegetation.

The Locust

One of the most destructive insects in the world is the locust, above. That is not to say that a single locust can do much damage. The problem is that they travel in swarms of hundreds of thousands of creatures. Such a swarm can devour hundreds of square miles of vegetation before it breaks up. This can spell disaster for farmers and may cause a famine in the affected area.

Locusts are, in fact, a very large species of grasshopper which live in the warmer parts of the world. Normally they are content to stay near their home area but every few years they will swarm. It is thought that the urge to swarm is caused by a dramatic increase in population, but scientists are not really sure.

What is known for certain is the devastation that a swarm can cause. Whenever a swarm nears, the farmers try desperately to drive the insects away.

Index to illustrations

Emu

Kangaroo

Animals from the Australian outback. See page 8.

Wombat